How Can
I Live without
My Baby?

Eulie R Brannan

WESTBOW
PRESS®
A DIVISION OF THOMAS NELSON
& ZONDERVAN

WestBow Press books may be ordered through booksellers or by contacting:

WestBow Press
A Division of Thomas Nelson & Zondervan
1663 Liberty Drive
Bloomington, IN 47403
www.westbowpress.com
844-714-3454

Unless marked otherwise, all scripture quotations are taken from the New King James Version®. Copyright © 1982 by Thomas Nelson. Used by permission. All rights reserved.

Scripture quotations marked NIV are taken from The Holy Bible, New International Version®, NIV® Copyright © 1973, 1978, 1984, 2011 by Biblica, Inc.® Used by permission. All rights reserved worldwide.

ISBN: 978-1-9736-9922-4 (sc)
ISBN: 978-1-9736-9923-1 (hc)
ISBN: 978-1-9736-9921-7 (e)

Library of Congress Control Number: 2023909757

Print information available on the last page.

WestBow Press rev. date: 5/31/2023

This book is dedicated to sufferers who hopefully will benefit by it. Take the Lord with you on your journey.

CONTENTS

PREFACE

Fifteen years ago, I was at the Huntsville Hospital visiting two friends who were meeting with a surgeon to discuss the plans for her surgery. An announcement came over the public address system for chaplains to please report to the cafeteria at once. When we assembled, they told us a bus filled with schoolchildren had just gone over a guardrail and fallen forty feet to the street below. Parents of the children had been asked to come to the cafeteria to learn about the condition of their children. Many parents had already assembled. I was asked to take a mother whose child was on the bus, and they showed us the room where we were to wait.

I tried to calm the mother by prayer and quoting scripture. She was so anxious she couldn't be still. When I saw the look on the face of the assistant hospital administrator, I knew the news would not be good. She closed the door and quietly told the mother, "Your daughter is dead." I will never forget the mother's reaction. She screamed, "Oh Jesus, I know you don't make mistakes, but how can I live without my baby!" This was a cry for help. "Oh Jesus, help me live without my baby!"

Her cry was a mixture of belief and unbelief. There was a man who came to Jesus pleading with Him to cast the demon out of his son.

> Jesus said, "If you can believe, all things are possible to him who believes." Immediately the father of the child cried out and said with tears, "Lord, I believe; help my unbelief!" (Mark 9:23–24)

Many sufferers have cried out for relief with the cry "I believe; help my unbelief."

INTRODUCTION

When I concluded my fourth book, I was talking with my daughter in New York. I told her I did not have any subject in mind about a fifth book. She said, "Dad, why don't you write about how you have been able to overcome loss? You have had a lot of losses; still, you have a bright, optimistic attitude. I believe many who have suffered or are suffering loss will be helped by reading how you have faced loss and overcame."

When I thought about it, I decided it would be worth relating times in my life that I don't visit very often. The book has been written with tears, but if it helps other sufferers, it will be worth the effort.

There are many kinds of losses suffered in this world, but I have centered on one type of loss. This writing has centered on the loss of a loved one close to you. All but one chapter relates my personal losses. Chapter 2 discusses the death of a child. Thankfully, this loss I have been spared. My wife had no miscarriages, and our four children are living and in good health.

1

I Am Acquainted with Grief

Dad's last nineteen days were spent in a nursing home. Hospice had not been established at that time. One of his pleasures was listening to music on a small transistor radio he kept on his pillow. He especially liked to hear Glen Campbell.

Early Experiences with Death

Death of My Best Friend

My first encounter with death came when I was fifteen years old. Larry was my best friend. We were together often, but when I went to school in Montgomery, we were able to see each other only occasionally. One day a teacher at the school told me he was going to Cullman for the weekend and invited me to go with him, which I gladly did. I always stayed with an aunt in Cullman. When I put my things up, I asked her permission to use the phone to call Larry. She turned pale. She said, "Didn't you know Larry died?" I was stunned.

When I regained my composure, she said, "I thought you had come for the funeral." Larry had gone swimming in a pasture pond and cut his foot on a tin can. They thought it would soon heal until they saw red streaks in the skin. Blood poisoning had set in, and the doctors could not save him. For the first time, I realized youth has no guarantee of life.

Death of My Grandmother

My next encounter with death came about two years after Larry's death. My maternal grandmother died, and I was asked to be a pallbearer. She was seventy-eight years old and considered to be advanced in age. That year, the average life expectancy for a woman was a little over sixty-four years. In a span of two years, I saw death come with a youth and an elderly lady. Job said, "Man who is born of woman Is of few days and full of trouble" (Job 14:1).

THE FIRST FUNERAL I PREACHED

The first funeral I preached was one of the saddest. It was for my friend who was in his twenties and had a wife and three children. I visited him in the hospital just before he died. He asked me to promise I would see his family was taken care of; I promised. From this I learned not to make promises I could not keep. I was in college and delivered over four hundred newspapers each morning before class. I had to do this to provide for my wife and son. In addition, I preached each Sunday. There was no way I could keep up with his family. I did for six months, and when they seemed to be provided for by her parents, I stopped.

At the funeral, his wife and three children were on the front seat. I waited for the funeral director to close the casket before beginning the service. When he removed the casket cover and started to close the lid, their five-year-old son pulled free from his mother's hands and rushed to the casket. He lay across under the lid so they could not close the casket. The son was loudly crying and shouting, "I want to see my daddy! I want my daddy!" This continued for five minutes before his mother could take him back to his seat. You can imagine the difficulty I had beginning the service.

The Death of My Father

When my father died at the age of sixty-five, death became very real. Dad was reared on a large farm his father owned, but I don't think he ever loved farming. At the age of twenty, he joined the navy and spent four years seeing the world. When his enlistment was over, he returned to the farm. He dated my mom for some time. It was ten miles between their homes. He would drive his buggy over, and when he came home, he let the horse lead the buggy home while he slept on the seat until the horse stopped at the barn.

They married, and Granddad gave them forty acres of land and a house. Not many harvests later, a bad crop year prompted Dad to say, "Let's sell out and go somewhere else. Where would you like to go?"

Mom said, "I haven't been anywhere; you have been everywhere. Where would you like to go?"

They went to Norwood, Ohio, where I was born. One year after my birth came the stock market crash of 1929, and the Great Depression began.

We went back to my granddad's farm, and Dad farmed for four years. Franklin Roosevelt became president, and his New Deal program began to get people back to work. Dad got a job with Fisher Body; when they shut down, he got a job at a card company. When this company closed, Dad's brother-in-law said, "Come to Huntsville; there are plenty of jobs." We moved and found the brother-in-law had lost his job. We moved to Atlanta, where Dad got a job as a night watchman for a construction company. He then applied for and finally got a job with Tennessee Coal and Iron (TCI) in Birmingham. When I finished the school year in Birmingham, I had attended five schools that year.

Finally, Dad had a permanent job, and we could settle down. Unfortunately, that did not come to pass. He worked the night shift at TCI, and one night we were awakened by two policemen who told us Dad had a bad car accident on his way home. They took Mom to the hospital where she learned they did not expect Dad to live. He had a fractured skull, his left arm was crushed, and there were other factures. He did survive, though he was in the hospital for six months; his left arm was more like a pectoral fin than an arm.

One thing I learned about Dad was he would work at any honorable job that would help him support his family. I saw him plow with two mules and one arm with the lines tied and looped around his shoulders. He worked from daylight to dark for fifty cents. He worked with WPA for $8 a week. World War II freed him from these low-paying, menial jobs.

When it was apparent America would be drawn into Hitler's war, production of domestic goods stopped and the companies began manufacturing ships, planes, tanks, guns, and other military equipment. Men were drafted or enlisted into the military, producing a great need for workers in these companies. Dad, with his handicap, was able to get a job at the shipyards in Mobile. Our personal economic condition greatly improved.

After the war, Dad moved to Cullman to help his father raise broiler chickens and became a part of the fast-growing chicken industry. When Granddad died, Dad moved to Montgomery, where I lived. Some of the most enjoyable years for him and Mom followed. They developed four routes in Lowndes County to sell Watkins products. The two would go together, and the business was so productive they ultimately worked only one week a month. During this time, he was an elder in the church.

These enjoyable years did not last long. Dad really liked parched peanuts and ate many as they made their rounds. When he developed a severe pain in his stomach, he thought it was from eating too many peanuts. Dr. Jackson ran tests and determined he needed to have his gallbladder removed. When Dr. Jackson performed the surgery, he found all the organs in the abdominal area were infected with cancer. He told Mom and me but not Dad.

When he and Mom were by themselves, Dad said, "It is cancer, isn't it?"

Mom said, "Yes, but how did you know?"

He said, "It wasn't what you said but what you didn't say." When the doctor came by, Dad asked, "How much longer do I have?"

Dr. Jackson said, "I think about six months."

During those six months, Dad had weeks when he visited family and friends and weeks when he was in bed. One thing he wanted to do was make sure Mom was taken care of when he was gone. They owned their house debt free and had savings. They had their Jeep station wagon they used for their routes and a family car. Dad wanted to leave Mom a new car. I had a good friend who was a Chevrolet dealer; we took the two vehicles and traded for a new Chevrolet for Mom.

During the final days of his life, I am sure the nurses gave him morphine to deaden the pain. The morphine caused him to be suspicious. Three days before he died, I went to see him and heard him screaming at a nurse as I was approaching his room. I entered the room, and with tears in his eyes, he said, "Son, tell them to stop poisoning me. I haven't done anything to them!"

I told him, "I'm here to protect you. Don't worry." I was able to calm him, but I knew the end was near.

The family was allowed to see his body at the funeral home. When I saw him, I was so glad those preparing the body were able to place the optimistic smile on his face that he'd had almost all the time. I thought, *Dad, you have been through a lot, but you never gave up or lost your optimism.* Many friends and family came to pay their respects to Dad and the family.

After his passing, I realized how much I missed his wisdom. During his life, I could always get him to evaluate my plans. I also thought of many things I wanted to know about the Brannan family that I wished I had asked him. One day I will have the opportunity to get my questions answered.

The Death of My Mother

No husband could wish for a better wife than my mom or a child for a better mother. She, like my dad, came from a large family and grew up on a farm. Dad had four brothers and three sisters; Mom had four sisters and two brothers. When she married, she vowed to Dad, like Ruth of the Bible, "Wherever you go, I will go; and wherever you lodge, I will lodge" (Ruth 1:16). You read about Dad's many travels and the different places he lived. Mom followed Dad without complaining and made the best adjustments possible for the family. She was a happy person and sang most of the time. My brother and I would get her to sing to us. I think I got my love for music from her.

There were times when Dad dealt with personal struggles; Mom took charge of the spiritual welfare of the family. Going to church services was not an option for us. We got ready for church because we knew Mom expected us to go. One time we had no available transportation, not even a mule and wagon. We lived about three miles from the church building. Olin, my older brother, was fourteen years old, and I was twelve. Our younger brother was three, and our sister was one year old. We walked to the church building with Olin and me taking turns carrying our brother on our backs and Mom carrying the baby in her arms. Sometimes one of the members would bring us home. If not, we walked. Olin and I complained but learned an unforgettable lesson about faithful church attendance.

Mom lived thirty-three years as a widow until her death at ninety-six. I smile when I think how my brother and I asked for her car keys when she had a fender bender at age seventy. She was getting very lonely living by herself, so I bought a duplex. She sold her house and moved into one apartment of the duplex, and I rented the other apartment to a young couple who treated her like a mother. This helped cure her loneliness.

The greater change came when Violet, her youngest sister who was living in Cincinnati, lost her husband. The couple in the other apartment informed me they had bought a place of their own and would be moving. Mom persuaded Violet to come and live in the vacant apartment. She was a godsend! She was full of life and said, "Come on, Bernie. We are going places." One time when I called Mom to ask how they were doing, she said, "Resting now. We walked down to visit the old folks at the nursing home." The nursing home was about five blocks from their duplex.

Another time they informed me they had bus tickets to visit a cousin in Idaho and then take a trip to San Diego to visit the zoo. One of their adventures at the zoo was riding the camels. It took them three days to get home from San Diego. When I asked if they got tired, they said, "No. We sat in the seat behind the drivers, and they looked after us. We enjoyed many meals at the bus stops along the way. It was fun." When Mom was eighty-two and Violet was seventy-three, I took them on a two-week trip to the Holy Land and three European countries. They talked about that trip the rest of their lives.

I kept getting reports about Mom falling, but she had strong bones and had not broken any bones with her falls. I knew it was time to get Mom and Violet in a safer place. I had heard about the Angels for the Elderly, where the elderly were cared for as long as they could dress themselves and were mobile. It sounded ideal to me. After I told them about the Angels for the Elderly facility, we went to visit it. They were told they could have adjacent rooms. Violet said, "We'll take them." We visited on Friday, and they moved on Monday.

They loved their new home. They had each other and quickly made friends with the other tenants. My brother Don, who lived in Montgomery, took them to church services. Mom was ninety years old when they went there, and she was able to enjoy four years. When she was unable to take care of her personal needs, we had to move her to a nursing home. Violet visited her almost daily, and Don went by several times a week. I was living in Madison and went to see her every time I was in Montgomery. Besides not being with Violet, the greatest thing she missed was not being able to attend church services. She was no longer able to get into Don's car. A preacher conducted a service at the nursing home each week, but it was not like attending her home church.

Though she was prepared, Mom never liked to talk about death. I said to her one time, "Mom, tell me what arrangements you would like for your funeral." She answered, "I have taken care of that. Violet and I prepaid all our funeral expenses." I said, "That's not what I meant. Who would you like to preach your funeral?" She replied, "I thought you three boys might say a few words, if you are still around." That was the end of the matter. A memorial service was conducted by her local preacher in Montgomery before we took her body to a country cemetery near Cullman, where Dad and many relatives were buried. Olin, Don, and I stood before her open grave and gave our fondest memories of Mom and commented on a few scriptures. She and Dad were together again after thirty-three years, surrounded by a host of relatives who had gone before.

Five years later, I held Violet's hand as she passed from time to eternity. She was able to stay at the Angels for the Elderly until she died. We took her to the same country cemetery, and I told of her good life and the home prepared for her.

The Death of My Older Brother, Olin

When Olin was born in 1926 prematurely, he only weighed two pounds. His survival was a marvel because not many preemies survived during that time. He was two years older than me and was both my provider and tormentor. He loved to aggravate me, but no one else dared to do that if he was around. When I was in the fourth grade, grades one through six were on the playground at the same time. A boy who was known to be a bully threatened me, but I said, "See that boy over there in the sixth grade. If you don't leave me alone, I'll call him over here and he will take care of you." That was the last time the bully bothered me.

Although he was my protector on occasions, he was my tormentor. Olin and I were going to visit some of our cousins using our usual means of transportation, our two feet. The road had been freshly covered with crushed flint stone. Olin found a wood shingle and suggested we pass the time taking turns hitting the rocks. We played pitch and bat with the rocks. This was great fun, and the time and distance passed quickly. Until I hit a rock that bounced off his head! He felt blood on his forehead and shouted, "You did that on purpose! I'm going to get you!" And he came running toward me. You don't know how fast you can run until you really need to run. I outran him, and as I topped the hill near my uncle's house, I was hollering, "Help!" My aunt caught him and put some disinfectant on his cut forehead, and he calmed down.

Mom wanted Olin and me to attend the Christian boarding school near Valdosta, Georgia. They did not have enough money to send both of us together for the fall semester. I was able to attend with him during the spring semester. After three weeks, he came to my room and asked me, "Do you like it here?" I said, "Yes." He said, "Would you stay if I were not here?" "Yes," I said, "but you are going to be here." "I may not," he said. "I have to face the discipline committee in the morning." He had been putting pennies behind the main fuse to shut off the dormitory lights so we could have pillow fights in the dark. Someone had hit our aged dorm supervisor in the head and knocked him down. He demanded the superintendent correct the situation. Olin went home.

Enough about Olin the boy. When he went home, he worked at the shipyard for a year and then enlisted in the navy. He was sent to the South Pacific to fight Japan. His ship was torpedoed, and he suffered a head wound that bothered him the rest of his life.

When the war was over, he married Jewel, and they would have five children. He had not completed high school, and I urged him to take the GED exam and enroll in college. He did so, and after completing two years of college, he joined the corps of engineers. He became a specialist in generating hydroelectric power and managed several plants. He was always active in the church and served as an elder in three different congregations.

Later in life Olin had Parkinson's disease. He lived in Pensacola, and I had relocated to Huntsville. He had a son in Huntsville, and during one of his visits with his son, Olin came to see me. I took him to lunch and realized how much the disease had affected him. He told me, "You will have to let me hold on to your arm and cut up my meat for me." Tears came to my eyes as I heard my big, strong brother ask me to cut up his meat. That was the last time I saw him before I drove to Pensacola to assist with his funeral.

The Death of My Younger Brother, Don

Don was nine years younger than me and was a late bloomer. He played in high school, dropped out before graduating, and joined the Navy. When he was discharged, he returned home a wiser, more mature man. He got a job where he met and married Dixie. They have two children.

I urged him to take the GED test and enroll in college. He did and earned a BS and an MS and finished his classwork for a PhD in mathematics. He taught math classes for me when I was president of the Alabama Christian College. He was very active in the church and became an elder in the same congregation where my dad had served for seventeen years.

Don had cancer and Parkinson's disease. He dealt with a weakened condition and pain for the last several years before he died at the age of eighty-two. He is survived by Dixie and their two children. Since I was ninety-one at the time of his death, I only was able to bid him farewell and listen as his minister and good friend delivered the eulogy. He was buried in the Greenwood Cemetery, where one day my body will be laid to rest.

I Am the Sole Survivor

During the writing of this book, my only sister, Jan, who was eleven years younger than me, passed away. I am the last leaf on the Olin H. Brannan family tree.

2

WHEN I BURIED MY SON,
I BURIED MY FUTURE

On the morning of February 6, 1991, Dennis Apple
discovered the lifeless body of his son on their family room
couch. Eighteen-year-old Denny had died. Dennis said,
"When I buried my son, I buried my future." (Dennis L.
Apple, *Life after the Death of My Son*, p. 81).

PERSONAL EXPERIENCES

I am grateful that I have been spared the grief of burying
one of my children. My writing will be based on knowing
the sorrow of some who have not been spared and on my
research. If you are grieving the loss of a child, I ask you now
to read Genesis 22:1–14. God commanded Abraham, "Take
now your son, your only son Isaac, whom you love, and go to
the land of Moriah, and offer him there as a burnt offering
on one of the mountains of which I shall tell you" (Genesis
22:2). Abraham must have thought he was having a bad
dream. All of God's promises were based on Isaac, the son

Abraham had waited for for twenty-five years. Something's not right. God abhors human sacrifices, and He is asking me to kill my own son. The death of any child seems unnatural. But Abraham was commanded to kill his own son.

There is that breathtaking moment when Abraham raised his hand to kill his son. "The Angel of the Lord called to him from heaven and said, 'Abraham, Abraham!'" (Genesis 22:11). "'Do not lay your hand on the lad, or do anything to him'" (Genesis 22:12). "Yes," you say, "but Abraham came down from the mountain with his son, and mine is gone." True, but Abraham thought he was going to have to kill his son. Abraham offered up his son, "concluding that God was able to raise him up, even from the dead, from which he also received him in a figurative sense" (Hebrews 11:19).

Here is another example that matches your loss. The God who created the heavens and earth sent his one and only Son to be His sacrificial Lamb to take away the sins of the world. He could have done anything to save His Son, but He did nothing. He watched as they beat Him, scourged, blasphemed, and spat upon Him. When they stretched Jesus on that cross, God did not say, "Soldier, drop your hammer!" When His Son cried out in that darkened day, "My God, My God, why have You forsaken Me?" (Matthew 27:46), He gave no answer. He knew if he stopped the crucifixion, there would be no hope for our forgiveness.

A grieving mother asked Gus Nichols, "Where was God when my son died?" He answered, "The same place He was when His Son died."

My first experience with preaching a funeral for an infant was for the Rickmans' baby who was born with spina bifida.

She lived only two years, but no baby had more loving care while living than this little girl. I don't remember exactly what I said, but I must have referred to Christ's statement "Let the little children come to Me, and do not forbid them; for of such is the kingdom of heaven" (Matthew 19:14). I tried to comfort them with the reminder that this was not a permanent farewell but one day they would have her back in a land where there are no physical impediments. Perhaps the most we can say is "I am deeply sorrowful for your great loss."

Fortunately, I knew enough not to make the mistake one preacher did. He thought to bring comfort to a grieving mother by saying, "God needed another flower in His flower garden." The mother cried, "How could God be so selfish to take my only flower when he had so many?"

A preacher friend named Jack Exam recounted this incident in his life. He said, "We men are sometimes so dumb," and then related this incident. He and his wife were looking forward to the birth of their baby. They learned they were having a boy, and his wife named him Timothy, a name she loved. Something went wrong and the baby was aborted. When Jack went to his wife's room, she was crying and said, "I always wanted to rear Timothy." In an effort to comfort her, Jack said, "Don't cry, and we will have another boy and name him Timothy." She almost shouted, "We will not! My Timothy is dead!" It makes a great difference when a living being has grown and developed as a part of the mother's body.

Another friend named Jack is a minister in Glasgow, Scotland. He and his wife learned they were going to have twin girls. The whole clan was excited because no one could remember the birth of twins in the entire clan. The twins seemed to develop normally until they stopped moving, and both were born dead. Jack and his brother placed the girls in small caskets and took them to the cemetery on the back seat of their car. Jack got down into the grave, and his brother handed him the caskets. From the grave, Jack tearfully cried, "Why, Lord?"

Jack could not sleep for six months. He went to the doctor and said, "Doctor, why did our twins die?" The doctor said, "I didn't want to tell you this, but the brains of the twins never developed. If they had lived, they would not live long, and you and your wife would have had to care for them twenty-four hours a day. You would not have been rewarded even with a meaningful smile." Jack said, "I could hear the Lord say to me, 'Jack, just take care of My business, and I will take care of your twins. One day I will give them back to you forever, whole and well.'"

BIBLE EXAMPLES

King David grieved the death of three of his children. A child was born to David and Bathsheba. Nathan told David the child would die. David pleaded for the child's life. For seven days, he would not eat, bathe, or change his clothes. When the child died, David bathed, put on clean clothes, went to the temple, and returned to his house to eat. His servants were astonished at his behavior. He answered, "While the child was alive, I fasted and wept. I said, 'Who can tell whether the Lord will be gracious to me, that the child may live?' But now he is dead; why should I fast? Can I bring him

back again? I shall go to him, but he shall not return to me"
(2 Samuel 12:22–23). That last sentence has brought comfort
to thousands who suffered the loss of a child.

The death of his son Amnon was the result of fratricide.
He was killed by his brother Absalom. Amnon thought he
was in love with Tamar, Absalom's sister and his half-sister.
He raped her and then threw her out of his house. "Then
Tamar put ashes on her head, and tore her robe of many
colors that was on her, and laid her hand on her head and
went away crying bitterly" (2 Samuel 13:19). She took refuge
in Absalom's house, and he pretended it was no great matter.
From that day, he planned the death of Amnon, and two
years later, he had his servants kill him.

Absalom fled to Geshur and was there three years (2
Samuel 13:38). Every day David longed to go to Absalom
but did not go. After three years, Absalom was brought back
to Jerusalem, but he did not see his father for another two
years. He had a charm his father could not resist. Absalom
returned determined to take his father's throne. David
seemed unaware until word came Absalom was marching
with an army from Hebron. He and those faithful to him
left Jerusalem immediately and established his headquarters
at Mahanaim.

David organized his army under the leadership of three
captains. Before sending them to the battle, he said, "Deal
gently for my sake with the young man Absalom" (2 Samuel
18:5). Absalom was killed, and that ended the rebellion.
Two runners wanted to take the news to David. One outran
the other, and David's first inquiry was "Is the young man
Absalom safe?" (2 Samuel 18:29). He either did not know

or chose to evade the question. The second runner was a Cushite who did not know or else did not care about David's love for Absalom. He shouted, "May the enemies of my lord the king, and all who rise against you to do harm, be like that young man!" (2 Samuel 18:32).

Here is the description of the king's reaction. "Then the king was deeply moved, and went up to the chamber over the gate, and wept. And as he went, he said thus: 'O my son Absalom—my son, my son Absalom—if only I had died in your place! O Absalom my son, my son!'" (2 Samuel 18:33).

Henry W. Longfellow's poem "The Chamber above the Gate" has immortalized David's sad lament.

> Is it so far from thee
> Thou canst no longer see,
> In the Chamber over the Gate,
> That old man desolate,
> Weeping and wailing sore
> For his son, who is no more?
> O Absalom, my son! …
> Somewhere at every hour
> The watchman on the tower
> Looks forth, and sees the fleet
> Approach of the hurrying feet
> Of messengers, that bear
> The tidings of despair.
> O Absalom, my son!
> That 't is a common grief
> Bringeth but slight relief;
> Ours is the bitterest loss,

Ours is the heaviest cross;
And forever the cry will be
"Would God I had died for thee,
O Absalom, my son!"

The action of a determined mother is related in 2 Kings
4:8–37. The prophet Elisha and his servant passed regularly
through Shunem. A notable woman there invited them to eat
at her house. This became a regular practice. Knowing Elisha
was a man of God, she persuaded her husband, saying, "Make
a small upper room on the wall; and let us put a bed for him
there, and a table too and a chair and a lampstand; so it will be,
whenever he comes to us, he can turn in there" (2 Kings 4:10).
Elisha enjoyed this accommodation and asked the woman
what he could do for her. She said she needed nothing. His
servant Gehazi learned that she wanted a son. Elijah promised
her that the next year she would have a son, and she did.

Tragedy struck. The boy went to his father, who was with
the reapers in the field, and said, "My head, my head!" (2
Kings 4:19). The father had servants take him to his mother.
She knelt by his bed until noon when he died. She took him
and laid him on the prophet's bed. A loving mother will do
anything for her child. She saddled a donkey and said to her
servant, "Drive and go forward; do not slacken the pace for
me unless I tell you." And so she departed and went to the
man of God at Mount Carmel (2 Kings 4:24–25).

Elisha saw her coming and knew something was wrong.
She fell at his feet crying, and the prophet knew something
was wrong with her son. He instructed Gehazi to take his
staff and lay it on the boy's face. This was not enough for this

mother. She said, "As the Lord lives, and as your soul lives, I will not leave you" (2 Kings 4:30). He followed her to her house and found the boy lying on his bed. He closed the door and healed her son. So he called her and said, "Pick up your son." So she went in, fell at his feet, and bowed to the ground; then she picked up her son and went out" (2 Kings 4:36–37).

Mark relates a sad scene in the ministry of Jesus as He showed His compassion and power to a distraught mother. As He and His disciples approached the small town of Nain, they saw a funeral procession. A dead man was carried out followed by his mother and many friends from the city. He was the only son of this woman who had lost her husband. Jesus had compassion on her and told her not to weep. He stopped the procession and said, "Young man, I say to you, arise." The man sat up. "And He presented him to his mother" (Luke 7:14, 15). How wonderful. "We do not have a High Priest who cannot sympathize with our weaknesses, but was in all points tempted as we are, yet without sin" (Hebrews 4:15).

The death of a child is unnatural. We want to cry out, "Something is wrong. It's not supposed to be like this!" The psychologist Carl Jung said, "The death of a child is like a period placed before the end of the sentence." Croesus, king of Lydia, said to Cyrus the Great, "Men would be fools to choose war. In times of peace sons bury their fathers; in time of war fathers bury their sons" *(The Histories of Herodotus)*.

We must learn to live with loss. Job lost his wealth and his ten children. He mourned sitting in sackcloth and ashes yet said, "Naked I came from my mother's womb, and naked shall I return there. The Lord gave, and the Lord has taken away; blessed be the name of the Lord" (Job 1:21).

One never gets over the death of a child; one just learns to live with it. When Jacob thought his son Joseph had been killed by a wild beast, his children tried to comfort him. He said, "I shall go down into the grave to my son in mourning" (Genesis 37:35).

SUGGESTIONS

Not having to suffer the death of a child disqualifies me from relating personal experiences. Instead, I will give you some suggestions from those who have suffered such a loss.

- Grieving parents will not want to hear this, but your family is changed forever; it will never be the same. You must find a "new normal." The journey is long and will take more time than you think you can stand. When Dennis Apple and his wife, Beulah, were barely surviving the death of their eighteen-year-old son, a woman said to them, "Hang in there; the second year is often worse than the first" (ibid., p. 12). This sounded almost unbelievable, given the suffering they were going through. But they found it was five years before they could begin to put the pieces back together again.

- You alone will have to work through your grief, but you don't have to do it alone. Perhaps this was Paul's meaning when he wrote to the Galatians, "Bear one another's burdens, and so fulfill the law of Christ" (Galatians 6:2). "For each one shall bear his own load" (Galatians 6:5). Also, you have God's unfailing promise "I will never leave you nor forsake you" (Hebrews 13:5).

The Dead Sea has no outlet except up. Through centuries, the sun has drawn the water to the sky, leaving deposits that made up potash that is the key ingredient of fertilizer. It is estimated if all the potash in and around the Dead Sea could be mined, it would be enough to cover the entire earth for five times. When we have no place to look but up, we can be richly rewarded.

- Those who have suffered the loss of a child say this death is the worst loss they have suffered. Someone said, "When I lost my parents, I lost my past. When I lost my spouse, I lost my present. When I lost my child, I lost my future" (Madd.org). We have a concern about the legacy we will leave. When we lose a child, we have lost an important part of our legacy.

- Time with your efforts will bring better days. John Claypool said, "Just like a broken leg, a heart heals slowly and cannot stand much touching soon after the break" (John R. Claypool, *Tracks of a fellow struggler*, XV). He saw his daughter Laura Lue suffer for two years before she died. Sometimes it seems so unfair. One sick child lives and another dies. Jim McGuiggan wrote, "There are few things that test our faith more than God changing everything for others and changing nothing for us" (Jim McGuiggan, *The*

God of the Towel, p. 165) How can you learn to live
with the pain?

In one day, Job lost his wealth and his ten children. His
response was

> Naked I came from my mother's womb,
> And naked shall I return there.
> The Lord gave, and the Lord has taken away;
> Blessed be the name of the Lord (Job 1:21).

His health was taken from him; he was covered with
painful boils from the crown of his head to the soles of his
feet. Even his wife turned on him.

> Then his wife said to him, "Do you still hold
> fast to your integrity? Curse God and die!" But
> he said to her, "You speak as one of the foolish
> women speaks. Shall we indeed accept good
> from God, and shall we not accept adversity?"
> (Job 2:9–10)

Three friends came to comfort him but became his
accusers. They accused him of being responsible for all the
disasters because of his sinning against God. Job protested
his innocence. He wanted an answer to a question all suffers
want to know. "Why?"

> Oh, that I had one to hear me!
> Here is my mark.
> Oh, that the Almighty would answer me,

That my Prosecutor had written a book!
(Job 31:35)

The Almighty did speak with him but did not tell him why bad things had happened to him. In the presence of God, Job said,

> Behold, I am vile; What shall I answer You?
> I lay my hand over my mouth. Once I have spoken, but I will not answer; Yes, twice, but I will proceed no further. (Job 40:4–5)

> Oh, the depth of the riches both of the wisdom and knowledge of God! How unsearchable are His judgments and His ways past finding out! (Romans 11:33).

Most Found Relief When They Were Grateful for the Time They Had with Their Child

- The Apples' son died twenty-four days before his nineteenth birthday. Instead of great joy, there was gloom that day. Dennis asked his wife, "Honey, if you had known nineteen years ago he would not live to see his nineteenth birthday, would you have wanted to give birth to him, raise him, only to lose him like this and experience this nightmare?" Through her tears, she said, "Oh yes, a thousand times over, I would do it all over again" (Apple, p. 98).

- John Claypool came to the point in his grief over the death of his daughter he could write this.
  I have two alternatives. I can dwell on the fact that she has been taken away, and dissolve in remorse that all this is gone forever. Or, focusing on the wonder she was ever given at all, I can resolve to be grateful that we shared life, even for an all too short ten years. There are only two choices here, but believe me, the best way out for me is the way of gratitude. (Claypool, p. 65)

- Edgar A. Guest lost two children. He regarded them as gifts, loans, from God in his poem "A Child of Mine."

I will lend you, for a little time, A child of mine, He said. For you to love the while he lives, And mourn for when he's dead. But should the angels call for him, Much sooner than we've planned. We'll brave the bitter grief that comes, And try to understand.

3

MY HARDEST BLOW

Merle Moore and I started courting in high school, and two years later, we decided we wanted to get married. I proposed, and she accepted with one requirement. I had to ask for her father's consent. I tried to prepare for all his objections. "You are too young." "Can you provide for her?" "Where will you live?" "Can she complete her senior year in high school?" I was a freshman in college. I prepared answers for all of his objections, and one Sunday afternoon, my opportunity arrived. Nervously I said, "Brother Moore, Merle and I are in love and want to get married. May we have your permission?" I was ready for everything but his reply. "It's all right with me. Just be good to her." We were married December 16, 1945, both at the age of seventeen.

I bought a twenty-six-foot house trailer for us to live in. Our budget allotment for groceries was $5 a week. Fifteen months after we married, Steve was born. Merle had graduated from high school, and I continued in college. Eighteen months after Steve, Deborah was born, and four years later, Rebecca was born. We had some hard financial months, but they did not seem hard because of our love for each other.

For the first fifteen years of our marriage, I was going to school. I received a BA degree from Huntingdon College, an MS from Auburn University, and a doctor of education from Auburn University. Merle did not return to pursue a college degree until our third child was in kindergarten. When she graduated from Huntingdon College, she received the Margaret Reed medal for the graduate with the highest grade average. Our children were with me at the graduation. When the announcement was made that Merle received the scholarship medal, our son Steve stood up and shouted, "That's my mother!" to the enjoyment of the audience. She continued her schooling to earn a master's degree and a year beyond a master's degree from Auburn University. The year 1960 was special for our family. We moved into a new house, she graduated from Huntingdon, and I received my doctorate at Auburn.

When I applied for a loan to buy our new house, I reported to the Equitable Life agent our family income. When I gave Merle's salary, he said, "We can only count one half of her income." I asked, "Why?" He said, "Women do get pregnant, you know." I confidently said, "We're both thirty-six and have our family." A year and a half later, the doctor said to my wife, "You're pregnant." Julie was a surprise and was born ten years after Becky. These once were referred to as "change of life babies." We were happy to welcome her into our family. Fortunately, Merle's mother was free, and we paid her to come and keep Julie during the time Merle was in school. This helped her mother and us.

Life was good. Our three older children had graduated from college and were married. Merle had advanced from teaching in an elementary school to being an administrator. She was assistant principal at the largest elementary school in Montgomery, and I was president of the Alabama Christian College, now Faulkner University.

In March 1980, I conducted a weekend seminar on marriage at Lakeland, Florida. When I returned home, Merle told me she did not feel well. We arranged to see Dr. Penton, our family doctor, the next day. He arranged for her to be in the hospital for a week to give her a battery of tests. Still, he could not make a positive diagnosis. He thought she had a collagen vascular disease, but he could not identify the specific one. His guess was rheumatoid arthritis. We were shocked, but he said, "This is probably the least debilitating of the group."

Merle kept on teaching but had to use many of her sick days. She had to go to the hospital a second time, and we decided she could not continue teaching. She had enough vacation days to be paid to the end of the school year and resigned her promised job as the principal of a new elementary school. She was in Jackson's Hospital in August, and I learned the importance of regular kidney monitoring. Dr. Penton said that if her creatinine level went above a certain mark, he was going to transfer her to the University Hospital in Birmingham.

Tine Davis, senior vice president of the Wynn-Dixie Corporation, was a friend of mine and great benefactor of the college. He had previously allowed me to fly on his jet to Jacksonville when he had a meeting of the corporation board to conduct business for the college. There was a bank president in Jacksonville I was cultivating to make a sizable donation to the college. I told Tine my friend had died of a heart attack, and there was another man in Jacksonville I needed to meet. Tine said, "I'm going Wednesday, and you are welcome to fly with me." I told him I needed to learn more about the new man before I went to see him. That Wednesday, Tine flew to Jacksonville with two of his executives and the two pilots. The five had dinner together, and Tine said, "I feel tired and am going to my room." The men went by his room about 10:00 to check on him and found him dead.

I was asked to be an honorary pallbearer at his funeral. When I returned to the hospital from his funeral, there was an urgent message on the speaker system for me to see Dr. Penton at once. He told me Merle's kidney levels were so high he was immediately sending her to the UAB in Birmingham. I followed the ambulance to Birmingham; every time it pulled to the side of the road and stopped, I thought there was an emergency.

When she was settled in her room, I drove back to Montgomery for clothes and other necessities. A friend had insisted I stay with him and his wife when I was in Birmingham. What value true friends are!

The test routine began again. Three or four days after we were there, the doctor ordered a dialysis treatment. After that four-hour ordeal, Merle said, "I had rather die rather go through that every week." That was the last dialysis treatment she had.

Early each morning I was in her room to get reports from her doctors. The main one came in with a serious look on his face and he said, "Our tests reveal she has scleroderma," a disease I had never heard about. He said it is a group of rare diseases that involve the hardening and tightening of the skin and connective tissues.

We were to see how true that is. I went to the hospital's medical library to learn more about the disease and its treatment. I learned much was not known about the disease and its treatment. Most of what was known about the disease was from postmortem examinations.

After three weeks in UAB, we were able to go home. I was given a strict diet with food that had to be weighed to be sure to have the right amount. I bought a balance scale and weighed portions for each meal, but she did not improve. She would be in Jackson's Hospital for a week and then home for a week. In the middle of September, she went back to Jackson's Hospital and could not improve enough to return home. Dr. Penton told me, "We don't have the equipment to administer dialysis, so I am transferring her to St. Margaret's Hospital, where they are able to give her treatments."

By this time, she had a rash all over her body that caused her skin to blister, die, and then peel off. Even the skin on the palms of her hands and the soles of her feet came off. I was in her room one morning and peeled the last dead skin off her body. I told her, "Look! You now have the skin of an eighteen-year-old girl." She had borne all this with remarkable courage. "Good! I can't bear this again," she said. We hugged, and both of us had big smiles on our faces.

The next morning when I went into her room, she was crying. I said, "What's wrong?" She just held her arm up, and it was covered with a rash that developed overnight. She was taken to the intensive care ward. I knew it was time to call the children home to see their mom. Steve and his wife drove in from South Dakota, and Becky came up from New Orleans. Debbie lived in Montgomery, and Julie was at home with me.

They took turns going to see Merle at visiting hours. On Tuesday night, an emergency arose. The disease had attacked her heart. All of us went to the hospital while the doctors worked with her. About midnight I suggested they go home, and I would stay until the crisis was over. I wanted Julie to get some sleep since she had to go to school the next day.

I waited in a designated area, and about three in the morning, the pulmonologist came to see me. He said, "I think we have pulled her through this bout, but you should expect this to happen time and again until she dies." Even after all we had been through, for the first time I thought Merle might have only ten or fifteen years to live. Sometimes when we want something to happen so badly, we cannot see obvious signs that what we want will not be.

On Friday night, Julie wanted me to go with her to see her high school football team play, and Becky wanted to stay with Merle at the hospital. Soon after we returned from the football game, Becky came home. She said Merle had been quiet and unresponsive, but the nurse said it would be all right if she went home. Steve and Julie went to the hospital to see her. Only a few minutes after they came home, we received an urgent call from the hospital for us to hurry to the hospital because Merle had taken a turn for the worse.

We rushed to the hospital, and the nurse said Merle had died. While we were still in shock, the nurse asked if we wanted to see her. Of course, we wanted to see her. I have heard preachers, including me, say, "That is only a shell; the spirit has departed." That's true, but I have never talked about what we did today or hugged and kissed a spirit. This ended our happy thirty-four years of marriage.

I am glad we will have a body in heaven. It will not be the same as this worn-out body. We will be changed. Paul wrote,

> The body is sown in corruption, it is raised in incorruption. It is sown in dishonor, it is raised in glory. It is sown in weakness, it is raised in power. It is sown a natural body, it is raised a spiritual body. There is a natural body, and there is a spiritual body. (1 Corinthians 15:42–44).

We want to know what this body will look like. John said, "Beloved, now we are children of God; and it has not yet been revealed what we shall be, but we know that when He is revealed, we shall be like Him, for we shall see Him as He is" (1 John 3:2). I know the all-powerful God has prepared the best body possible for His Son. To know I will be like Him is enough for me.

We went into a room, and Merle looked like she was peacefully asleep. I can even now clearly picture how beautiful she looked, even in death. The designated funeral home came for her body, and we went home. I don't remember how long we stayed up or if I slept any that night.

The next morning, I called the funeral home for an appointment to make arrangements for the funeral. Debbie, Julie, and I went to make the arrangements. The place was to be at the home's large auditorium, and the time was ten on Monday morning. They explained the cost for their services, and then came the hard part, selecting the casket. I had helped many people when their loved ones died. At that time, I had never helped anyone select a casket. We went into a room with low lights shining and beautiful, soft music playing in the background. Three of the walls were lined with caskets and a double row in the middle of the room. Plackets were on the top of each casket giving the price and special features. After selecting the one we wanted, we selected the guest book and thank-you notes.

The home representative totaled the cost, and we gave him some insurance policies that covered all the expenses. The owner of the funeral home sent me word he wanted to donate the cost of opening and closing the grave in honor of Merle. This gesture was greatly appreciated. We went home to get the clothes we wanted her to wear, a copy of the obituary we wanted put in the newspaper, and to order the number of death notices we wanted. Fortunately, he insisted on more than we thought we would need. Heed the undertaker's advice.

The time for the visitation was approaching; the family was given the opportunity to see Merle first. She looked beautiful and was only fifty-two years old. We went into a reserved room; the casket was opened, and the casket cover was arranged. I stood at the head of the casket with one of my children beside me, and the other three with their spouses stood at the foot. The doors were opened for friends and well-wishers to come in. They kept coming until the line was stopped at fifteen minutes before the funeral was to begin. We were given time to say our last goodbyes, and then the casket was closed and rolled into the auditorium. Brother VP Black made a few remarks and led a prayer. We all filed into the auditorium.

Brother Black gave a beautiful tribute to Merle and reminded us of that wonderful land to which she had gone. The college chorus sang some songs. They sang "Peace, Perfect Peace" that became Steve's favorite hymnal during his year's deployment in Vietnam. I had attended the funeral of Don Morris, president of Abilene Christian College, and the college chorus sang a special arrangement of "Shall We Gather at the River?" their choral director had arranged. It was so beautiful that I asked our choral director for our chorus to sing it at Merle's funeral.

This is a time when your faith is so very important. We got into cars and went to the gravesite. A tent had been set up for the immediate family and elderly who could not stand. Brother Black's remarks were brief. I don't remember a thing he said. Remember the grieving may not remember a thing you said, but they will never forget you cared. We were asked to wait in our cars until the grave was dressed. When we went back to the grave, the casket had been lowered into the vault and covered. The mound of dirt was gone, and the gravesite was covered with some of the floral tributes. The friends left and we went home.

How wonderful to find the college cafeteria had prepared a delicious meal, and they were ready to serve us. We were exhausted but very hungry. The out-of-town children had to leave to get back to work. Soon it was Julie and me in the 8,500-square feet president's home.

Merle and I enjoyed the *All in the Family* weekly comedy TV show. It featured Archie Bunker and his wife, Edith. Stern Archie treated Edith more like his servant than his wife. In the last episode, Edith died. The stoic Archie determined to show no emotion. A night or two after her death, he went into the bedroom on her side of the bed and saw her house shoes under the bed where she always kept them. He picked up one, his eyes filled with tears, and fell across the bed crying and sobbing.

I shed some tears when Merle died but was determined not to lose it. I wanted the children, especially Julie, to know I was going to be all right. Our bed was positioned so I had to go by Merle's side to get to our private bathroom. I happened to look back at Merle's side one night and saw her house shoes neatly positioned under the bed where she always kept them. I could barely stand up but fell across the bed and cried until there were no more tears to shed.

How do you get over a loss like that? If that means "How do you forget about it?" my answer is "Never." Merle died over forty-one years ago, and I have had to stop my typing and wipe tears from my eyes when composing this account. If you mean "How do you process and live with it?" I will tell you in a later chapter what has helped me.

4

ANOTHER HARD BLOW

When I became the president of a Christian college, it was struggling with a heavy debt burden. In my first meeting with the board, the chairman asked me, "How do you propose we raise $300,000 in the next two months?" This amount was needed to show a balance sheet that would qualify us to negotiate a new bond issue. We had a great board, and I said, "It must begin in this room." They responded by pledging to give $120,000 within sixty days. One board member, VP Black, a great friend of the college, was given a leave of absence by his church to work with me in raising the money.

We were able to raise the money, and this convinced us we could avoid the expense of a new bond issue. One of our board members worked for the largest bank in Montgomery. I asked him to arrange a luncheon for us with a vice president of the bank who was a supporter of the college. He and I had become friends, and I wanted to tell him how much we could save by avoiding a new bond issue. I wanted then to suggest we could have a fund drive to pay the three banks what we owed them. In addition, the college had to pay the

$400,000 due in four months for a balloon payment coming due on the original bond issue. This balloon payment was a part of the original bond issue that enabled the college to move to a new campus.

My thought was to ask him for a large lead gift to launch the campaign. The VP said nothing and was scribbling on a pad while I talked. When I finished, he said, "You cannot have a successful drive now; your donors are tired." Turning to the bank employee, he said, "Charlie, why don't we see if the three banks they owe would get together and lend the college enough to pay off the banks and the bond payment? They would have the collateral of the retired bonds." Charlie said, "I don't think they will agree." He said, "We won't know until we try. I will talk with our president to see if we will be the lead bank."

The three banks did lend the college a million dollars with $92,000 payments due every six months. I give these details to say I was getting tired of the struggle. We made seventeen of those semiannual payments over the next eight and a half years, but each one was a struggle. When Merle died, I was very tired of the struggle. I had dealt with debts so long I could not dream about expansion and additional debt.

After Merle's death, a lady called to give me her condolence for my wife's death. She was a member of the Governor's Women Commission, and the commission had inspected the conditions at the women's prison in Wetumpka. I had met Willie Metta Strong about ten years earlier when I conducted a meeting in Huntsville. When she called, I was in a meeting with my vice presidents and told her if she would give me her number, I would call that night. I called and that was the first of many calls.

We did not get together until I was going to Nashville to give the commencement address at David Lipscomb College. Our friendship grew into love, I proposed marriage, and she accepted. I resigned as president of the college, and we were married by my brother in her daughter's living room in Atlanta. I was scheduled to speak at a National Education Forum the next week in New Orleans with Dr. George Benson, president of that organization. The program was sponsored by the civic clubs of New Orleans. We spent our honeymoon at the Roosevelt Hotel, which was not what Willie Metta would have chosen.

TRINITY TERM AT OXFORD UNIVERSITY

For some time, I had wanted to see what the British education was like. Oxford University is a combination of thirty-nine colleges. I had applied for admission and was accepted by Manchester College, founded in 1786. After six weeks of marriage, we boarded a plane for the Heathrow Airport in London. We had five large suitcases with our belongings for three months.

At the airport were no porters to help with our luggage. Fortunately, the train to Oxford came through the terminal. I put one suitcase under my arm and two in my hands, Willie Metta carried two, and we made our way to board the train. The local minister had invited us to stay with him until we found a place for ourselves and promised to meet us at the train station. I called from London to tell him when we would arrive.

I had never met John, the minister, and would not recognize him at the train station. I kept looking for someone looking for an arrival, but I saw no one. I called John's house, and he answered the phone, surprised that we were already at the station. He and his daughter came to get us. When I saw his minicar, I thought there was no way four people and five large suitcases could get in it. We did so by all but the driver sitting on a suitcase. It was cold and had started sleeting. When we were about a half mile from his house, his car ran out of gas. We sloshed through the sleet to his house carrying the suitcases.

John was very hospitable, but no one was prepared for the weather. That night we used all the cover for the bed and laid our winter coats over the covers, and still were cold. We heard thunder, and blue lightning streaked across the sky. Willie Metta could not sleep and went to the window to see the weather. See said, "It's snowing outside." I said, "It can't be with all the lightning." I went to the window and saw a solid sheet of snow falling.

The next morning, six to eight inches of snow were on the ground. The weather bureau reported this was the worst April snow in one hundred years. John had cooked a roast for our lunch when we came home from church services; I looked at a thermometer on a shelf and the temperature was fifty-three degrees. John had only one fireplace. His big dog lay in front of it and growled at anyone who came near.

When we were by ourselves, Willie Metta said, "Let's go home." I said, "I can't. I'm enrolled for classes. But I will get you a ticket." That afternoon she was on the phone with the airport asking when she could she get a flight back to Atlanta. Divine providence spared me. You may recall in April 1982 the airport control tower operators threatened to go on strike. President Reagan said, "If you do, I will fire all of you." They went on strike, and he fired all of them. When she called about a flight, she was told there were no flights going in or out of the American airports.

I told John, "Let's go looking for us for a place to stay before I lose my wife." We went to Queens College, and I inquired at the housing department. The lady said, "We don't have any student housing available." I said, "I don't want student housing. My wife is with me, and I am enrolled as a professor on sabbatical." She said, "How much can you pay?" I said, "What it takes." She said, "Let me take you to Admiral Jamison's office. He is responsible for all housing assignments." When I explained what I wanted, he said, "Professor Thompson is on sabbatical and will be back in July." I told him that would fit my schedule since we were returning to the States the end of June."

He called his assistant to take us to see the apartment. It was very nice with central heat. I called Willie Metta to see if she wanted John to take her to see the apartment. She said, "Is it warm?" I said, "Yes." She said, "Take it!" I made proper arrangements, and we moved in the next morning. Willie Metta was warm for the first time since we left the train station.

She enjoyed the rest of our stay except for a sick spell. The doctor wanted to remove her gallbladder. She refused, telling him she was taking her gallbladder home with her, which she did, and she still had it when she passed away.

Sometimes there was a language barrier. The oven of the stove stopped heating. She called the building superintendent and told him she needed a repairman. She said, "The stove oven won't heat up." He asked, "The what?" She repeated and said, "The stove where you bake the bread." He said, "Oh, the cooker." The language was not exactly our English. We had to learn what the boot, bonnet, and windshield were on an automobile.

When I rented the flat, Admiral Jamison said, "You will get a monthly utility bill, except for the tele. When you know when you are leaving, I will get the utility bill for you." That day came, and I called Admiral Jamison. He came out to the flat. He said, "Oh professor, this tele bill is beastly, beastly." I asked him how much and gave the amount in pounds, which was about $1,800. I told him that was about what I expected. Willie Metta called her daughter in Atlanta and my mother in Montgomery about every day. The admiral walked away mumbling, "Beastly, beastly."

ACADEMIC EXPERIENCES

I was enrolled as a professor on sabbatical, which entitled me to attend any class in any of the thirty-nine colleges. I chose eight classes, one in archaeology, one on the Reformation, and the others in studies of biblical texts. Some of the teachers, like at most universities, were excellent, and others were ordinary. The week I attended, the Barret Lectureship was interesting. Barrett was a wealthy gentleman who died at the turn of the twentieth century leaving the university a large sum to establish an annual lectureship in his name. The object was to get an outstanding scholar to speak each year. The one scheduled to speak the year I was there had two PhDs, one in Bible and the other in Near Eastern affairs.

I asked where I could apply to get a ticket to attend and was told to just show up. I knew it would be held in one of the large auditoriums available but was surprised when it was held in a classroom seating about one hundred. On the first day, about seventy attended, including most of my professors. I wanted to take in all he said so I sat on the first row with pen in hand to make copious notes.

I listened to hear his main points but heard none. That afternoon I bought a recorder to record his lectures and listened to them a second time when I returned to our flat. This continued all week. When the last lecture was over, I was thinking how stupid I must be. One of my professors, Chesley Jones, boarded a bus with me and we sat down. He turned to me and said, "I'll say, the ole boy was a bit foggy." I smiled and gave him a vigorous handshake.

Interesting social occasions were the high dinners on Friday nights. The faculty met at seven for thirty minutes to get acquainted and drinks. They thought we were strange to just drink Cokes. Everyone was seated at the table next to someone other than their spouse. A five-course dinner was served with glasses of drinks. One night Willie Metta was seated across the table from me, and I could hear her conversation. She was seated by a female doctor who had just returned from India and was talking about their overpopulation. She then got on birth control. I held my breath hoping she would not ask Willie Metta her opinion. She said, "I think abortion is the only solution, don't you Mrs. Brannan?" Willie Metta said, "No, I don't. I think abortion is sinful." The doctor mumbled, said, "That is one view," and changed the subject.

Another night she was seated by a young man who was on the staff of a member of the House of Lords. He talked about many subjects, including gun control. At that time, the English bobbies did not carry guns. He said, "Mrs. Brannan, don't you think it is a shame the way you Yanks have so many guns?" She said, "No, I don't. I carry my thirty-eight in my purse all the time when I'm home." He quickly looked at his watch, said, "It's getting late. I'm off," and left.

BACK HOME AND NO JOB

At the end of the semester, we returned to the States. I faced a need I had not experienced before. I had never needed to look for a job. I searched about a month for a job. I had several places that had tried to hire me when I had a job, but now when I needed a job, they had no openings. It was good for me because it helped me to develop empathy for those out of work. Dr. George Benson, former longtime president of Harding College, was founder and president of the National Education Program. This organization was dedicated to presenting the principles that made America great. He needed a field director. I interviewed, and he hired me.

My job was to speak at as many civic clubs as I could and emphasize that America was founded on three fundamental principles: faith in God, constitutional government, and private ownership of property and businesses. I also arranged dinners sponsored by prominent individuals in the city for him to speak. He had a powerful, compelling speech. I followed up the meeting by calling on the attendees to ask them to support the NEP.

BACK IN CHRISTIAN EDUCATION

I had been field director for a year when Dr. Frank Sutton asked me to have lunch with him. He had been a great help during Merle's fight with scleroderma. Dr. Sutton was chairman of the board of a Christian academy in Birmingham. He said they were looking for a president and wanted to know if I would be interested. After talking with Willie Metta, I took the job, and we moved to Birmingham. We made many lifetime friends while in Birmingham. While I was president of the Christian academy, we established a congregation on campus and moved to a new campus.

CHANGE OF CAREER

While president of the Christian academy, I was invited to speak on a forum in Atlanta on institutional development. The main speaker was the president of an institutional development firm in Memphis. I spoke on cultivating large donors. I told Rob, the president of the company, "I would like one day to join a development firm." He said, "Let me know when you are ready, and I think I can use you." After seven years at the Christian academy, I was tired of balancing the budget. In November of my eighth year, I called Rob and told him at the end of the school year I would be ready, if he had an opening. He said, "Call me then, and I am ready." I informed my board so they could search for a replacement.

In the middle of the next month, Rob called and asked if I could join his firm the first of January. He had a new client that was thinking about a major fund drive, and he needed me to do a feasibility study. I had a capable young assistant whom I recommended the board select as president, and I would help him at no charge one week each month until the end of the school year. They agreed, and I joined Rob's firm the first of January.

BACK AT ALABAMA CHRISTIAN COLLEGE

I was surprised to learn that Rob's new client was the college I left nine years before. The study involved interviewing the board members and other good friends of the college to see what amount was reasonable for a fund drive and how much they would be willing to give. Since I knew all the board members and most of their close friends, this was an enjoyable experience. I wrote the results of the study and our recommendation for the fund drive. Rob met with the board, and they agreed to hire us for sixteen months to organize and give counsel for the fund drive. The fund drive was successful, and at the end of our contract, the college president hired me to be his special counsel to the president.

When I knew I would be working for the college, I asked Willie Metta where she wanted to live. She said, "I want to go home," and we made plans to move to Madison. I had not realized the sacrifice Willie Metta made going with me to Oxford and especially moving to Birmingham. In May we moved to Madison. For the next fourteen years, almost every week I would leave Madison early on Monday morning for Montgomery and return Thursday night. These were enjoyable years, and I made lifelong friends. David Short, VP for advancement, and I traveled thousands of miles together. I continue to regard him as one of my best friends. I saw the college advance beyond my dreams.

Willie Metta developed a stomach problem that she was sure was cancer since her mother had died from stomach cancer. I knew I had to be at home more. As I pondered how I could continue to work for the college and be at home each night, Mike Winkler, the minister of the Madison Church of Christ, asked me to have lunch with him. We met for lunch, and he said, "The elders are looking for someone to work with me to keep from losing members. They asked me to ask you if you would be interested." I told him to let me talk with Willie Metta and the college president. Willie Metta gave an enthusiastic yes. I talked with the president, and he expressed regret that I would leave, but he understood.

I talked with the elders, and we agreed on a work contract. One month later, I stopped work for the college on Friday and began work with the church on the next Monday.

Fourteen years of very enjoyable work at the Madison church followed, until I resigned at the age of eighty-eight.

Willie Metta did not have cancer but a bacterial infection that was very difficult to kill. She enjoyed five more years of good health but began to have ministrokes. One Sunday afternoon, she was sitting at the table and suddenly could not move or speak. I called her son, David, and we had her taken to the emergency room, where she was diagnosed with a major stroke. After two weeks, the hospital wanted her moved to another facility.

An incident occurred that grieves me to think about. We had agreed neither of us would allow the other to be put in a nursing home. When the doctor came by her room, her daughter, son, and I asked the doctor to join us in an adjacent room so we could talk privately. We wanted him to get a place for her in the best rehabilitation facility in the city. He agreed. When we came back to her room, I noted a troubled look on her face. Later when her son and I had left, she told her daughter she thought we were talking about sending her to a nursing home.

She was in rehab for four weeks. Our Christmas was spent sitting in her room and reminiscing. When she was released from the rehabilitation facility, we hired three sitters to be with her around the clock. We knew if she fell, her daughter and I would be unable to get her up. She continued rehabilitation until she could show no improvement. It was time to call in hospice. They were wonderful.

On a Monday evening in May, we rolled her to the dinner table, but she refused to eat anything. We told the hospice nurse, and she said, "Don't try to force her to eat; she is doing her death work."

A remarkable thing happened on Wednesday. She had been totally unresponsive, but David came and sat on the side of her bed. He spoke to her, her eyes opened, and they talked and laughed about humorous events in their past. When he left, she lapsed back into unconsciousness and early Friday morning died peacefully. I gently rubbed my hand across her face to close her eyelids. Hospice came and immediately took over. This was two months before her eighty-eighth birthday.

The next morning, we went to the funeral home, where she had prepaid her funeral expenses. The funeral was planned for the next Monday with visitation at ten and the funeral at eleven. Many signed the guest book that could not stay for the funeral, but the auditorium was filled. Our two ministers were wonderful in their remarks. Willie Metta had said, "No funeral possession to the cemetery. It is too dangerous." The family ate a delicious meal the church had prepared and then at two thirty gathered for a private funeral service at the Maple Hill Cemetery. As Solomon said, the body returned to the dust and the spirit to God who gave it (Ecclesiastes 12:7). This ended our thirty-one happy years of marriage.

5

The God of the Good Old Days Is Also the God of the Good New Days

I don't know anyone who has suffered the losses the Old Testament patriarch Job endured. He was a righteous man and "the greatest of all the people of the East" (Job 1:3). In one day, he lost his ten children and all his great wealth. His camels, oxen, and donkeys were stolen, and his sheep died in a fire. He said, "The Lord gave, and the Lord has taken away; Blessed be the name of the Lord" (Job 1:21).

Job was struck

> with painful boils from the sole of his foot to the crown of his head. And he took for himself a potsherd with which to scrape himself while he sat in the midst of the ashes. (Job 2:7–8)

Even his wife added to his pain, saying,

> "Do you still hold fast to your integrity? Curse
> God and die!" But he said to her, "You speak
> as one of the foolish women speaks. Shall we
> indeed accept good from God, and shall we
> not accept adversity?" (Job 2:9–10).

Three friends came to comfort him but became his accusers when he refused to admit his misfortune was caused by some great sin he had committed and refused to confess. Former associates who held him in high honor turned against him. "I am one mocked by his friends" (Job 12:4). Some of the vilest mocked him. "But now they mock at me, men younger than I, Whose fathers I disdained to put with the dogs of my flock" (Job 30:1).

Given his dire constancies, he did what most in similar situations will do. He thought about the good old days. "Oh, that I were as in months past, as in the days when God watched over me" (Job 29:2).

> When I went out to the gate by the city,
> When I took my seat in the open square,
> The young men saw me and hid, And the
> aged arose and stood; The princes refrained
> from talking, And put their hand on their
> mouth; The voice of nobles was hushed, And
> their tongue stuck to the roof of their mouth
> (Job 29:7–10)

I chose the way for them, and sat as chief;
So I dwelt as a king in the army, As one who
comforts mourners. (Job 29:25)

Such memories are pleasant and good unless one dwells in the past and refuses to think about today and the future. Max Lucado was quoted as saying, "Gratitude lifts our eyes off the things we lack so we might see the blessings we possess." Paul had great successes and miserable failures in his past. He said,

Brethren, I do not count myself to have apprehended; but one thing I do, forgetting those things which are behind and reaching forward to those things which are ahead, I press toward the goal for the prize of the upward call of God in Christ Jesus. (Philippians 3:13–14)

Job thought if he could just see God, He would explain why his life had been wrecked. God did appear to him and bombarded him with questions he could not answer, and he came to understand he could not fathom God's way. God did not answer his why but showed him that the God of the good old days could be the God of the good new days.

God blessed Job in his latter days more than his beginning. He had twice the wealth and seven sons and three daughters. "In all the land were found no women so beautiful as the daughters of Job; and their father gave them an inheritance among their brothers" (Job 42:15). Job lived another "one hundred and forty years, and saw his children and grandchildren for four generations" (Job 42:16).

His ten new children did not replace the ten he had lost. For one to appreciate the good new days, one must be flexible enough to hold the past as beautiful memories while opening one's eyes to the good new days.

I HAVE SEEN THE GOD OF THE GOOD OLD DAYS IS ALSO THE GOD OF THE GOOD NEW DAYS

When Willie Metta died, I was eighty-three years old. The Lord had blessed me with two good wives, and I thought I did not need another. I filled my life with activities. I was still employed full time with the Madison church as the associate minister. Almost every morning, I had a sausage biscuit and coffee with a friend at the neighborhood Burger King. Some mornings were with the same friends each week, and others were with different ones who wanted to talk with me. The Burger King became like the place on *Cheers* where "everyone knows your name."

This was very enjoyable, but at night, while others went home to their families, I went home to an empty house. Though I had read about it, I was surprised that the loneliness hit me so hard six months after Willie Metta's death. I often would wake up in the middle of the night and automatically reach over to touch her, but she was not there. Or I would get up to go to the bathroom thinking I had to be quiet to keep from waking her. Then I would realize she was not there and would not be there anymore. When I finished my day at the office, I would come home and we would sit in our lounge chairs and discuss our day's activities. I continued to come home and rest in my lounge chair, and sometimes when I looked at her chair, I thought I saw her sitting there.

A little more than a year after her death, I realized I wanted someone to love who might also love me. Then we would spend the rest of our days together. One Sunday morning before services, I asked my stepson to come by my office for a minute. I said, "David, I'm terribly lonely, and I am going to see if I can find another good wife." You dog lovers will understand his language. David has always loved dogs and has two. He said, "If Jan (his wife) died, I don't know if I would want to housebreak another wife." Of course, he was saying adjusting to any marriage relationship is difficult. I laughed, took off my wedding band Willie Metta had given me thirty-two years before, and gave it to him.

DUSTING OFF AN OLD SKILL

I had not courted for decades. How would I begin? My children saw my loneliness and were eager to help me. Two of my daughters thought a popular online dating service would be a good way to start. They said, "We will pay for six months' membership and take care of everything." I agreed. One took several pictures of me to send in and filled out the questionnaire profile for me. She came to the question about age and asked, "What shall I put as your age?" I said, "How old am I?" She said, "Eighty-five." "That's what you put," I said. I soon saw that those who wanted an eighty-five-year-old man were not ones I wanted. I never answered an inquiry.

My son said, "I'm going to sign you up with a Church of Christ dating service." This did not have pictures, and I had to read the profiles and make a judgment. There was one who had an interesting profile, until I read, "I will not leave Oklahoma!" I knew I was not going to live in Oklahoma, so that service ended with no inquiry from me. I forgot about the dating services.

I realized I must find someone who shares my spiritual values and hope for eternity. This meant my best chance for a good marriage and a companion to the end of the way lay with finding someone I already knew. My thoughts immediately centered on Louise Wright. She had been a widow for five years. She is very attractive and eight years younger than me, so the chances I would have to bury a third wife were remote. Her late husband, George, was a good friend of mine; we had played golf together almost every week for several years, until he became too sick to play.

A SHAKY COURTSHIP

You know we men are afraid of rejection. I felt like an eighth grader asking for his first date when I called Louise to see if she would like to have dinner with me on Friday night. She said, yes, and I made a reservation for us at a nice restaurant. The night went well, and I suggested next Saturday we drive about forty miles to a Mennonite restaurant that had delicious home-style food. She agreed.

We talked on the phone one night that week and I said, "I think we must be totally honest with each other. I am looking for a good wife." She said, "Then you need not waste your money next Saturday; I do not plan to remarry." I said, "OK. I will give you a rain check." No date the next Saturday.

I continued to call her, and we talked a long time on the phone. She explained her condition. She had a beautiful home and sufficient finances to live comfortably the rest of her life. She has two sons who will give her all the help she needs, and one son's company was near to her house and he usually had lunch with her five days a week. I said, "Will you pray that I will find a good wife?" She agreed.

Our relationship almost ended. I called one Friday night, and she sounded nervous. I sensed someone was with her. I asked her if a man was there. She said, "Yes, I will call you later." I said, "Don't bother. I am not going to be in competition with anyone," and hung up. The next morning, she called me and said she had told her friend they had no future together. I told her, "Thanks for calling. Remember you have a rain check available any time you wish to cash it."

THINGS TURN FOR THE BETTER

My children gave me a birthday celebration for my eighty-fifth birthday on a Sunday afternoon at the Madison church building. It was well attended, and Louise came but I did not remember seeing her. A few Sundays later, we drove up for Sunday services at the same time. I said to her, "Remember you have a rain check any time you want to use it." She said, "I told you at your birthday celebration I was ready." I said, "I didn't hear you." The rain check was cashed the next Saturday.

We resumed our telephone conversations. Divine intervention made our conversations and dinners more serious. One night she hesitantly told me her experience. She said, "I was praying for the Lord to help you find a good wife and something happened that never happened before. The Lord stopped me when I made my request for you. I said, 'Not me, Lord.'" I immediately told her I wanted her to read in Isaiah 6:8 where the Lord said, "Whom shall I send, and who will go for us?" Then I said, "Here am I! Send me." I said, "You know you can't go against the will of the Lord." Our relationship then became serious.

We cashed her rain check at Outback. The first time we attended a church event was the Young at Heart banquet the young people provided for the older members. I can imagine a lot of the members began to wonder about us. We then started regularly going to church services together. Some of Louise's friends warned her she might be taking on a caregiver's role. On the night of my eighty-sixth birthday, I proposed, she accepted, and I placed her engagement ring on her finger.

The next decision was about our wedding. Neither of us wanted an elaborate church wedding. Who would we invite to a small wedding without offending some who were not invited? We decided to have a private wedding with only us, the minister, and two witnesses. At ten in the morning of May 6, 2015, Mike Winkler, minister of the Madison Church of Christ, with our family minister and a secretary as witnesses, joined us in the holy bond of matrimony. Louise's son Dwight had made her a beautiful corsage and me a pretty boutonniere.

We had discussed where we would live. Both of us had beautiful houses. Willie Metta and I each paid one half of the cost of our house. The deed had the provision that should one die, the survivor had the right of occupancy until their death, and then the property would be sold and the proceeds divided between the two families. This meant should I die before Louise, that is likely, she would be without a home. I agreed to sell my house, and she provided three rooms for me to put the furniture I wanted to take with me. We spent most of our honeymoon moving my things.

Louise had been married to George for over fifty years, and I had been married to two women for a total of sixty-five years. Two people with many similarities still have differences to deal with. Some we learn to resolve and others we accept. This is true of all marriages. A young couple recently married was eating breakfast, and the husband said, "Honey, you don't make biscuits like my mother did." She replied, "And you don't make dough like my dad did." Some things are better left unsaid.

Louise and I have not traveled very much. I was eighty-six and she was seventy-seven when we married. Travel is difficult: packing and carrying heavy bags, lots of walking, and some crooks are looking for the elderly as easy targets for robbery. When you have lived alone, you learn to appreciate the quiet things.

Just to know there is one in the house who loves you and you love her is comforting. We know if a health emergency occurs, one is ready to get necessary help. To prepare meals together, have conversation while eating, then cleaning up the dishes helps to bond the couple together. Louise is an outdoor lady and enjoys working in the yard and tending to her flowers. We both enjoy eating breakfast on the patio. We love looking at the beautiful landscape, watching the squirrels play, and hearing the birds sing. To have our evening devotional and read the newspaper together is enjoyable. We watch our favorite TV programs together.

Going to church services together and having fellowship with our friends is spiritually uplifting. We, like many others, did not realize how important this is until we had to miss getting together with fellow Christians for over a year because of the COVID pandemic. Fortunately, we had electronic facilities available to worship together online. Since the COVID pandemic has abated, we have been enjoying having a meal at a good restaurant.

Louise and I have children who provide a great support group. She has two sons who live within ten miles of our house who check on us all the time and will give us any help needed. I have a son one hundred miles and a daughter two hundred miles from us who come any time I need someone to go with me to see a doctor whose office is difficult to get to. We have church friends who will give us any help needed.

We also have our private time and space. I have my writing I enjoy. She enjoys talking with friends on the phone and is constantly doing things around the house. I take a nap almost every afternoon. I call it my minivacation. I haven't been able to persuade her of the value of it. Maybe in eight or nine years she will appreciate it.

We are fortunate that each of us has adequate financial resources that prevent us from worrying about finances. I cannot overemphasize the importance of saving sufficient resources for your latter years. If you live long enough, that time will come. Old age has enough health and other problems that you need to be free from worrying about paying your bills, if possible.

I know young people will not think our lifestyle is very exciting, but for us, it is comfortable and satisfying. Older folks will appreciate it. We consider ourselves very fortunate to have lived so long and are as active as we are.

WE HAVE HAD HEALTH CHALLENGES

Four days after my eightieth birthday, I had a triple bypass with open-heart surgery. Things went well, and I forgot about it after six months. I watch my eating habits, exercise regularly, and get adequate rest. I have annual visits with my cardiologist and thus far have heard the great news "See you next year." When I reached my ninetieth birthday, I told my doctor, "One day you will ask your nurse if it's not time for Mr. Brannan to come in for his annual checkup. She will check my file and tell you, 'Mr. Brannan is deceased.' When that happens, remember I'm in a better land where I will never need a doctor!'" I remind him of that each year.

I had my left knee replaced before we were married. A year after we married, my right knee was giving me so much trouble I went to see an orthopedic surgeon. He took x-rays and showed me I had no cartilage, but it was one bone on the other. He said, "You can have surgery now or suffer a little longer and then have it." I chose to have it then. All went well, and after ten days of rehab, I was able to walk by myself. I have found two artificial knees do not give me as good a sense of balance as my natural knees. I have fallen a few times but no serious injuries. Thank the Lord I am still vertical.

Several years ago, Louise had to have a pacemaker inserted to regulate her heart rhythm. She no longer notices it; however, every nine or ten years, she has to have the battery replaced. Not long after we married, she hit her sciatic nerve near where it enters the spinal column on a sharp counter corner. It caused her intense pain, and we went to Birmingham to an outstanding neurosurgeon. He surgically removed the pressure on the nerve and resolved her problem.

She also has had her right knee replaced like I did. She has always quickly recovered from these problems. I attribute this to three things. First is her optimistic spirit. Second is the way she has always taken care of her body. She has always been active, controlled her weight, and exercised regularly. She and George turned their garage into a minigym with a weight machine, treadmill, elliptical machine, and exercise bike. She uses these regularly. Third is the grace and care of God.

In 2018 she went for her annual mammogram expecting everything to be normal as usual. Since no one in her family had cancer, she had no great concern. The next day her doctor called and asked her to come to the office for a biopsy. He had found a small growth that did not look cancerous, but he wanted to be certain. He did a biopsy, and the lump tested positive for cancer. He then arranged surgery to have it removed. It was about half the size of a pea, and all the tissue and lymph nodes around it were clear.

As a precaution, she had twenty-one radiation treatments. She reported to an outstanding oncologist at the Clearview Cancer Clinic for regular evaluations. Everything was fine, and the thought of her cancer was at the back of our minds. Two years after having the lump removed, Louise was hospitalized with balance problems and mental confusion. Her oncologist was out of town but ordered a biopsy of her liver. She was given many different tests with all the results normal. She was scheduled to be released on Friday. Thursday night her oncologist returned and went to the hospital to read the results of her liver biopsy.

One of her sons stayed with her every night at the hospital. When her doctor came by the next morning, he had shocking news. Her breast cancer had metastasized and spread to the liver. He released her from the hospital that Friday but wanted to see her the next Monday to begin treatments. His goal has always been to give her a long life and good quality of life. The first few treatments hit her hard, until her body was able to adjust. The doctor has always been searching for new drugs that will be more effective in treating her cancer.

He has found a mixture of two drugs that prevents the cancer growth and produces few side effects. Louise is amazing. She comes home after her biweekly treatments full of energy and says she would not know she has cancer if the tests had not shown it. Others taking treatments are amazed and even doctors are impressed. Her normal routine is to go to the center, have blood drawn, see her oncologist or PA, and then have a three-hour infusion.

What does the future hold? We do not know what the future holds, but we know who holds the future. We both have lived a good long life and are prepared to go when the Lord calls. Our confidence is based on three undeniable facts: God loves us, He wants what is best for us, and He will do what is best for us. With confidence we say, "Father, not our will, but thine be done."

"To whom be the glory forever" (Romans 11:36). Amen.

6

How I Learned to Laugh Again

"Blessed are you who weep now, For you shall laugh" (Luke 6:21). My remarks may mean little to one who does not believe in life after death. When his daughter Sophie died, Sigmund Freud, an atheist, wrote to a friend that he had no one to blame and no place to go for comfort. Nine years later, his grief was as sharp as when his daughter died.

To Love Is to Risk

Every time we make the decision to love someone, we open ourselves to great suffering, because those we most love cause us not only great joy but also great pain. The greatest pain comes from leaving. The pain of the leaving can tear us apart. Still, if we want to avoid the suffering of leaving, we will never experience the joy of loving. And love is stronger than fear, life stronger than death, hope stronger than despair. We have to trust that the risk of loving is always worth taking. (Henri Nouwen Quotes, internet).

I have dared to risk loving more than once and found the risk worth the suffering when death took my beloved from me. Some of those occasions have been described. I have been asked, "How have you been able to overcome the sorrow and laugh again?" To me life is not worth living without loving. Paul wrote, "Now abide faith, hope, love, these three; but the greatest of these is love" (1 Corinthians 13:13). Here are several things that have helped me.

I HAD TO FACE THE FACT MY LOVED ONE IS DEAD

I can cry, "I don't want her to die. I need her. She is too young. It's not fair." I still have to face the fact my loved one is dead and is not coming back. I have a friend whose stepfather died, and his wife refused for over two years to move his bathrobe from the chair by the bed or the clothes he was planning to wear hanging on a door. She refused to fully accept the fact he was dead. This only delays the grief process necessary for healing.

Moses was not permitted to take the children of Israel into the Promised Land, and Joshua was publicly introduced as his successor. The last time the Israelites saw Moses, he was ascending Mount Nebo to look at the Promised Land. Though he was 120 years old, he climbed with the strength of a young man and his eyesight as good as in his youth. No one saw his grave. God had to move

Joshua into action with the statement "Moses My servant is dead" (Joshua 1:2).

Elijah was one of God's greatest prophets. Elisha was with him when God took him to heaven in a whirlwind. The young prophets, who did not see him go, thought he might have been left on some mountain. They pleaded with Elisha to let them search for him. He tried to dissuade them but finally acquiesced. Fifty men searched for three days in vain. They had a hard time accepting the loss of Elijah.

You can shed copious tears, but you at some time have to accept the stark reality of your loss. Edgar Allan Poe's poem "The Raven" has the raven giving the solemn answer.

> Tell this soul with sorrow laden if, within the distant Aidenn, It shall clasp a sainted maiden whom the angels name Lenore— Clasp a rare and radiant maiden whom the angels name Lenore. Quoth the Raven "Nevermore."

ACCEPT THE WEIGHT OF YOUR LOSS

Dream about them. Wake up in the middle of the night and feel the other side of the bed to see if they are all right and find there's no one there. My wife and I sat in recliners by each other and talked about our day's work. I still sat in my recliner and sometimes looked over and saw her there, but she vanished. See someone and think, *I can't wait until I get home and say to her, "Guess who I saw today,"* but she's not at home to listen.

We used to watch the comedy *All in the Family*. In one of the last episodes, Edith died. Archie, the tough husband, showed no emotion. That night when he was going to bed, he went on Edith's side and saw her house shoes under the bed. He lost his control and cried like a baby. As referenced in an earlier chapter, the same thing happened to me. The smallest reminder can bring back memories, and the emotions flood in. It may be a song both loved or a seeing a place both enjoyed. Jennifer Williamson said, "We need to grieve the one we've lost—not to sustain our connection to suffering but to sustain our connection to love."

One important lesson I learned is my intellect is much quicker to accept the facts than are my emotions. Well-wishers will say, "She has gone to a better place." Others say, "You would not bring her back to her pain if you could." Yes, my mind is accepting these facts, but they do not relieve my loneliness or questions about my future. Probably one day they will, but not now. Asking why is asking what may only be revealed in eternity. God gives us this promise: "And we know that all things work together for good to those who love God, to those who are the called according to His purpose" (Romans 8:28). On that promise, we base our hope.

TIME WILL HELP TAKE THE RAWNESS OUT OF THE LOSS

Time does not erase the loss, nor would we want it to. Some unknown writer expressed it beautifully. "When we lose someone we love, we must learn not to live without them but to live with the love they left behind." Life goes on and demands our attention. This will help us one day to laugh again.

Each one grieves in their own way. There is no right way for everyone. All usually feel they have managed their grief and are surprised to have it return almost as strong as at first. I was surprised to have my grief return six months after my loss. This was especially true of my loneliness. This encourages some, as it did me, to be emboldened to think they may find another to help relieve the loneliness.

KEEP BUSY

When my wife died, I was associate minister at the Madison church. There were duties I had to do that others took for several days, but I needed to get back to work. That helped me with my grieving process. It kept me from having a lot of time to think about things I wish I had or had not done. I filled my schedule with having breakfast with friends for business, social, or Bible talk.

Keeping busy seems to help men more than woman, but knowing there was work waiting on me helped me get out of bed in the morning. You don't need to become a workaholic, but work and get tired enough that you don't think about your loss all the time.

DON'T ISOLATE YOURSELF, AND BE GRATEFUL

Wounded animals tend to get away from other animals and lick their wounds before returning to the group. We sometimes do the same. Since much of our grief is private and no one else can fully know the extent of it, we think we must bear it alone. Paul wrote to the Galatians, "For each one shall bear his own load" (Galatians 6:5).

Positive thinking is invaluable. Gratitude can work wonders with our attitude. I had nothing to do with my birth; it was God's gift. God gave me thirty-four years with Merle, my first wife, and thirty-one years with Willie Metta, my second wife. How fortunate I am to have that much time with two wonderful women. How could I ever be bitter that they were taken from me? We will do much to help our grieving if we can stop thinking so much about losing our loved one we had for a long period of time and be grateful we had them at all.

LET YOUR FRIENDS HELP

Psalm 41 was written when David's son Absalom was leading an army against him, trying to take his throne. His enemies were delighted. "All who hate me whisper together against me; Against me they devise my hurt" (Psalm 41:7). The hardest blow was delivered by one whom David considered his close friend. "Even my own familiar friend in whom I trusted, Who ate my bread, Has lifted up his heel against me" (Psalm 41:9). In contrast, Solomon said, "But there is a friend who sticks closer than a brother" (Proverbs 18:24).

A friend walks in when others walk out. When you are blinded by grief and don't know which way to turn, a friend takes you by the arm and guides you in the right way. They anticipate your needs even before you know you need them. They know when to speak and when to just be close by.

Helen Keller, who was both deaf and blind, said, "Walking with a friend in the dark is better than walking alone in the light."

DOES JESUS CARE? OH YES, HE CARES; HIS HEART IS TOUCHED WITH MY GRIEF

These words from the song "Does Jesus Care?" speak a great truth. Jesus shed tears three times: once for Himself and twice for others. His good friend Lazarus was dead. He went to Bethany to raise him from his grave. When He saw the anguish of Lazarus's sisters, Martha and Mary, whom He loved, John records, "Jesus wept" (John 11:35).

When Jesus was about to make His triumphal entry into Jerusalem, at the descent of the Mount of Olives He stopped. He saw the city and wept over it, saying,

> If you had known, even you, especially in this your day, the things that make for your peace! But now they are hidden from your eyes. For days will come upon you when your enemies will build an embankment around you, surround you and close you in on every side, and level you, and your children within you, to the ground; and they will not leave in you one stone upon another, because you did not know the time of your visitation. (Luke 19:41–44)

Jesus in His mind was seeing forty years into the future when the Roman army destroyed Jerusalem. The very valley they were about to cross would be filled with crosses with dead or nearly dead victims hanging on them. Starvation was so great that some mothers ate their own children. The sword, famine, or pestilence would wipe out most of the inhabitants of Jerusalem. Jesus could not envision this without shedding tears.

The one time He wept for himself was when He was alone with the Father in the Garden of Gethsemane. "He had offered up prayers and supplications, with vehement cries and tears to Him who was able to save Him from death, and was heard because of His godly fear" (Hebrews 5:7). God heard His plea, "Let this cup pass from me," (Matthew 26:39), but for our redemption, the Father had to reject His plea.

Another thing makes us certain Jesus cares about our sorrow is His compassion. On at least seven different occasions, He showed His compassion.

When Jesus went about all the cities and villages, He was compassionate with the multitudes "because they were weary and scattered like sheep having no shepherd" (Matthew 9:36).

When multitudes met Him when He had retreated with the apostles for rest, "He was moved with compassion for them, and healed their sick" (Matthew 14:14).

On another occasion, the multitude were with Him for three days without food. He had compassion on them, saying, "I do not want to send them away hungry, lest they faint on the way" (Matthew 15:32).

He had compassion on a wild man who could not be chained or controlled and cast the demons out of him (Mark 5:19).

Two blind men at Jericho who wanted their eyes opened came to Jesus. He had compassion on them and gave them their sight (Matthew 20:34).

A leper came to Him and said, "If You are willing, You can make me clean." Then Jesus, moved with compassion, stretched out His hand, touched him, and said to him, "I am willing; be cleansed" (Mark 1:40–41).

Jesus saw a widow following the casket holding her only son. "When He saw her, he had compassion on her" (Luke 7:13). He raised the boy from the dead and gave him back to his mother.

We can never doubt Jesus loves and cares for us.

GOD CARES FOR US

Many passages confirm this truth. Jesus told Thomas, "He who has seen Me has seen the Father" (John 14:9). Paul said, "He is the image of the invisible God" (Colossians 1:15). Knowing how Jesus reacted to the pain of others, we can know how God feels.

Try to imagine the feelings of God when He watched His Son being crucified.

In the Garden, He pleaded, with loud cries and tears, "Let this cup pass from me" (Matthew 26:39). His Father refused.

At the house of Caiaphas, they spat in His face, beat Him, blindfolded, Him, and slapped Him, saying, "Prophesy! Who is the one who struck You?" (Luke 22:64).

The Roman soldiers stripped His clothes from Him, put on a purple robe, platted a crown of thorns, placed it on His head, gave Him a reed as a scepter, and bowed down in mockery, saying, "Hail King of the Jews" (John 19:3). They then took the reed, beat him over the head, and put His clothes on Him and led Him to be crucified. His Father saw this. What did he do? Nothing!

Jesus apparently was too weak from the night's mistreatment to bear His cross all the way to Calvary, and Simon was compelled to help him. There they stretched Jesus across a cross, fastened his hands and feet to it with spikes, and placed it in the hole. For six hours He suffered, painfully drawing Himself up to get each breath. Even on the cross, He did not escape mockery from the thieves, the soldiers, and Jewish leaders who came to watch the spectacle.

The last three hours were shrouded in darkness, and in the darkness came Christ's despairing cry. "My God, My God, why have you forsaken me?" (Matthew 27:46). This must have brought tears to the Father's eyes, but He said nothing!

I had an experience that makes me think the Father's emotions were deeply stirred. When my oldest daughter, Debbie, was six, she had surgery on her eyes. The surgeon emphasized the compression bandage had to remain in place on her eyes for a day. When I went in to see her, she was lying on her back in a large crib bed with each hand tied to a side of the bed. The nurse explained the bandage hurt and each time her hands were free she would reach to pull it off.

When the nurse left the room, Debbie pleaded with me to untie her hands. I explained what the nurse had said and how even though it hurt, the bandage had to stay on for her eyes to heal correctly. She tearfully said, "Just untie one hand, and I promise not to touch the bandage." I said, "Are you sure?" She said, "Yes." I untied her left hand, and quick as a flash, it went for the bandage. I barely grabbed it before it reached the bandage. I had to force her hand back and tie it to the crib with her crying and resisting in every way. I then knew her instincts would immediately cause her to go for the bandage if her hand was free. I had to leave the room hearing her crying and pleading, "Daddy, please." Though it has been almost seventy years, tears fill my eyes as I write this.

Why did God not stop His Son's crucifixion? He had done no wrong. It was because He loves us so much. Christ alone was great enough for His death to atone for the sin of every believing sinner from Adam to the end of the world.

Knowing it was for you, God left His power unused to save Jesus from crucifixion. We are instructed to cast "all your care upon Him, for He cares for you" (1 Peter 5:7).

IN EVERYTHING GIVE THANKS

Is Paul asking the impossible of us when he says, "In everything give thanks; for this is the will of God in Christ Jesus for you" (1 Thessalonians 5:18)? How can we give thanks for our losses? How can I give thanks for the deaths of my two wives?

I can if I keep certain things in mind.

First, as a mortal man, I cannot expect to know the ways of God. His ways are "past finding out" (Romans 11:33). We will have to wait until we are in a better land to understand many things.

Second, I must know and believe the promises of God. He knows us, loves us, and will do what is best for us.

These three promises mean much to me.

1. He will not allow a heavier load to be laid on me than I can bear (1 Corinthians 10:13).
2. All things work for good to them that love the Lord and are called according to his purpose (Romans 8:28).
3. He will never leave us or forsake us (Hebrews 13:5).

Alford Lord Tennyson wrote "Crossing the Bar," which expresses my hope. Tennyson wrote this poem about three years before his death and requested it be placed at the end of every edition of his works.

> Sunset and evening star,
> And one clear call for me!
> And may there be no moaning of the bar,
> When I put out to sea,
> But such a tide as moving seems asleep,
> To full for sound and foam,
> When that which drew from out the boundless deep
> Turns again home.
> Twilight and evening bell,
> And after that the dark!
> And may there be no sadness of farewell,

When I embark;
For tho' from out our bourne of Time and Place
The flood may bear me far,
I hope to see my Pilot face to face
When I have cross'd the bar.

Epilogue

When my second wife, Willie Metta, passed away, I promised myself there would be no more marriages. I didn't think I could go through the grief process of burying another wife. I described in chapter 5 how loneliness overwhelmed me a year after her death. I told how Louise Wright and I came together. I was certain that her being almost nine years younger than me assured I would die first. For six years, this seemed certain. But I have learned that "a man's heart plans his way, But the Lord directs his steps" (Proverbs 16:9).

In October 2018, Louise went to get her annual mammogram. She expected to get a letter saying, "It looks good," as she had since she had begun the annual exams. She got a call from her doctor the next day saying he saw a small growth he wanted Dr. Robertson to biopsy. He said, "It's probably nothing, but we want to be safe." She thought, *No cause to worry because no one in my family had cancer.* The biopsy was positive for cancer, but the edges were clean, and two lymph nodes nearby were clear. Just to be safe, she was given twenty-one radiation treatments. We then forgot about cancer.

Two years later, she had to go to the hospital because of an imbalance and mental confusion. She stayed a week and was given all kinds of tests. Dr. McGee, her oncologist, was out of town but ordered a biopsy of her liver. On Friday he came by to check on the biopsy and gave us a shocking report. The cancer had metastasized to her liver. Without treatment, he gave her three to six months to live. With treatment, he thought he could give her one to two years. The treatments began the next Monday.

She had some hard times for the first year as Dr. McGee tried different chemo combinations. About eight months ago, he started an experimental treatment that used two different drugs. She would have blood drawn, see Dr. McGee, and get a three-hour infusion of the chemo. The next week, she would have blood drawn, talk with the nurse, and return home. The following week, she had blood drawn, saw Dr. McGee, and got a treatment. For about seven months, the combination held the cancer in check, and she had few side effects. She often said, "If the tests had not shown it, I would not know I had cancer."

What does the future hold?

James gave some very good advice regarding the future.

> Now listen, you who say, "Today or tomorrow we will go to this or that city, spend a year there, carry on business and make money." Why, you do not even know what will

happen tomorrow. What is your life? You are a mist that appears for a little while and then vanishes. Instead, you ought to say, "If it is the Lord's will, we will live and do this or that." (James 4:13–15 NIV)

We should always put a codicil to our statements about future plans: "If the Lord wills." When you are facing a fatal disease, it is a necessity. We talked about Thanksgiving, and I said, "Do you plan to do a lot of baking and prepare a lot of dishes as you and Dwight like to do or just order the meal for the family from Walton's restaurant like we did last year?" She wisely said, "I don't know. Let's wait and see." She will not be with us this Thanksgiving.

About a month ago, a scan revealed the cancer was spreading. She started a new, stronger treatment that required treatments once a week for two weeks and then a week off. She had her first treatment three weeks ago, and the next day became so weak she could not stand. She went to the hospital to get liquid infusions and came home after two days.

She took a second dose that had been reduced to half strength. For two days, she seemed to tolerate the treatment. But then she had complications. She contracted sepsis in the blood from a colon infection. Her A-fib caused her heart to race and her blood pressure to become unstable. She received four units of blood and an intravenous drip with antibiotics, fluids, and nourishment. She remains in the hospital with the future unknown (9/1/22).

The "Vale of Tears"

Almost fifty years ago, I attended a meeting of Christian college leaders at David Lipscomb College. Our luncheon speaker was Dr. Batsell Barrett Baxter, former head of the Lipscomb Bible department. He had to resign because of his cancer. He spoke about going for his treatments and witnessing the hallway lined with patients in wheelchairs waiting for their treatments. Many were sobbing, and he called the hallway a "vale of tears." These last two weeks have been a vale of tears for me.

September 2, 2022: We received shocking news this morning. Dr. McGee, her oncologist, came in and said, "Her liver has shut down. She has days, not weeks, to live." All attention has turned to palliative care. One of her two sons is with her twenty-four hours a day.

September 6, 22: Eight years ago on my eighty-sixth birthday, I gave her an engagement ring. Today on my ninety-fourth birthday is our eighth anniversary. Louise is struggling. Morphine and Ativan are administered regularly. Louise loves flowers. I console myself about her struggling with the thought that the Spirit has shown her heaven's flowers, and she is struggling to get there and tend to the flowers in heaven's Eden. We were talking about heaven one morning and she looked out the window and saw her beautiful flowers. She said, "I hope the Lord will give me the job of helping to take care of the flowers in heaven."

I received good news that she is being transferred to Hospice House this afternoon. No more intravenous drips and constant traffic to interfere with her rest. Only oxygen and pain medication are now administered.

September 7, 2022: Today at 1:00 p.m., Dwight is taking me to see Louise at Hospice House. They have put her on a stronger medication, Percocet. Hospice House is a beautiful place: light, airy, and very peaceful. Ernie greeted us, and we went to her room. The men left me alone with Louise. I sat beside her bed, and when I had gained control of my emotions, I talked a long time. I said, "Baby, this is ER, your husband." I think I saw a stir. She was breathing deeply. I told her yesterday was my ninety-fourth birthday, and it was on my eighty-sixth birthday eight years ago that I proposed to her and gave her the engagement ring. I rubbed my cheek across her arm and said, "I wanted you to know I am clean-shaven and know you would not want me with a briar-patched beard talking to you."

I then reviewed our courtship and marriage as described in chapter 5. The doctor came in and checked her, and I asked, "How long?" He said, "Only One knows for certain, but based on my experience, I would say she will be gone within the next twenty-four hours." I got up and placed my cheek next to hers and softly said, "Baby, it looks like this will be the last time we will be together in this world. But I will see you on the other side of Jordan. When I arrive, come out of your flower garden and greet me. Bye."

September 8, 2022: Still waiting. I have heard Louise say a hundred times, "I don't like being rushed." We got up at five on Sunday mornings to eat and get ready to leave at eight for our morning worship service.

September 9, 2022: Still waiting. Every time I receive a text, I think it is from Ernie or Dwight telling me the Lord has called Louise home.

September 10, 2022: My stepson David took me to Hospice House to see Louise this afternoon. She is still in this world. She had worried about me if she died first. We had discussed an independent living place near my daughter Debbie. I told her my son would take me to see it, and I am going to be all right. "You can stop worrying about me."

At the Madison church, we have a singing on fifth Sunday nights. She always wanted me to lead a song, but I told her there are too many good leaders for me to lead one. I said, "If I ever led one, it would be the one with these lyrics":

I have heard of a land on the far away strand, 'Tis a beautiful home of the soul; Built by Jesus on high, where we never shall die, 'Tis a land where we never grow old. Never grow old, never grow old, In a land where we'll never grow old.

The lyrics are from a song by James C. Moore. I then sang it to her. I hope she was able to hear.

September 11, 2022: Still waiting. Her sister and niece visited her.

September 12, 2022: Nurse said signs indicate she may pass today. It did not happen. "But those who wait on the Lord shall renew their strength" (Isaiah 40:31).

September 13, 2022: Nurse said, "Her pulse is weak and oxygen low; she will surely go today." She made it another day.

September 14, 2022: About 7:30 a.m., Dwight texted that her pulse was barely detectable. "Looks like she is about ready to go home." Dwight texted at 7:35 a.m., "She went to be at home with the Lord." I was standing when I read it and had to quickly sit down. I had expected it with every text or phone call for eight days, but the news opened a gate and a flood of emotions rushed out. I sobbed for several minutes before I could gain control.

The funeral service is arranged for Sunday afternoon, September 18, 2022.

September 18, 2022: Today has been a long, hard day. I attended the church service with Steve and Brenda, my son and daughter-in-law, and Debbie and Pat, my daughter and son-in-law. We hurried from the church to the funeral home. I approached Louise's casket with my daughter by my side. Louise was beautiful even in death, but the sight of her opened the floodgate of emotions and the emotions gushed out. When I gained control, I talked to her. I know she had been with the Lord four days, but this physical body was the only one I had talked with and hugged. I told her I would soon join her, and we could talk as long as we wished.

My son and daughter and their spouses, along with Louise's family, received friends and well-wishers extending their condolences from twelve thirty to two thirty. Then we went to Maple Hill Cemetery for the graveside service that Louise wanted. Brandon Pressnell delivered a beautiful eulogy about the worthy woman of Proverbs 31.

Then I heard a voice from heaven saying to me, "Write: 'Blessed are the dead who die in the Lord from now on.'" "Yes," says the Spirit, "that they may rest from their labors, and their works follow them." (Revelation 14:13)

The family went to our house for a delicious meal prepared by the ladies at the church. Louise's son, Dwight, is finishing cleaning up at nine o'clock. He is such a wonderful helper who wants everything just right, as his mother would. If she could see, I am sure she smiled her approval.

ANOTHER CHANGE

Change is never easy, and the older we get, the harder it is. Since I married my first wife seventy-seven years ago, I have made seven major changes. I am ninety-four years old, and it is not safe for me to live alone. I need to be close to my daughter who lives in Montgomery, and I have lived about half of my life in that city.

Yesterday, I was in Montgomery finalizing my plans to live in a two-bedroom suite at the Crossing, an independent living village only ten minutes from my daughter's house. What does the future hold? I don't know, but I believe the Lord will make it work out for my good.

Now to the King eternal, immortal, invisible, to God who alone is wise, be honor and glory forever and ever. Amen. (1 Timothy 1:17)

BIBLIOGRAPHY

Apple, Dennis L. *Life after the Death of My Son*. Kansas City: Beacon Hill Press, 2008.

Brecheisen, Jerry and Wilson, Lawrence W. *When Life Doesn't Turn Out the Way You Expect*. Kansas City: Beacon Press, 2003.

Claypool, John R. *Tracks of a Fellow Struggler*. New Orleans: The Inside Press, 2004.

Herodotus. *The Histories*. London and New York: MacMillan and Company, 1980.

McArthur, John. *Anxious for Nothing*. Colorado Springs: David C. Cook, 2012.

McGuiggan, Jim. *The God of the Towel*. West Monroe: The Howard Publishing Company, 1997.